Dedication

To Mother and Daddy for their support and love.
  To Joseph and Mary and the good Lord above.

To my family and friends and those still to meet.
  I love you all. You make me complete.

To teachers and students that Oodle's a source,
  to travel toward knowledge on a diligent course.

With special thanks and gratitude to Johnny Fo,
  and the tireless efforts of Nat and Jo.

  M.Y.

Have a great
TIME
travelling with Oodle MaDoodle!

2008

Library of Congress Card Number: 2001 135450
ISBN: 0-9704457-0-9
First Printing: November 2001

COPYRIGHT 2001

If this book is not available at your local bookstore, copies may be ordered directly from:

Chef John Folse & Company Publishing
2517 South Philippe Avenue
Gonzales, Louisiana 70737
(225) 644-6000
http://www.jfolse.com

Price: $15.95 plus $3.50 for shipping/handling ($19.45)

Story: Michaela D. York
Illustrations: Erik Van Buren
Edit: Michaela D. York and Natalie D. Aprill
Design: Jodi Conachen
Software: QuarkXpress
Hardware: IBM 44x Max
Printed in Canada

Mr.OodleMaDoodle's
Time Around The World

Story by Michaela D. York
Illustrated by Erik Van Buren

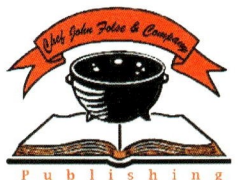

Chef John Folse & Company
Publishing

"I must grab my timeometer,
compass and maps,
paper and pens
and my duffel with straps."
Oodle MaDoodle knew well
today was today,
but why in Europe
it was tomorrow,
he couldn't yet say.

"Why does time differ as
you travel the globe?"
he wondered aloud
this question to probe.
Oodle hopped on his scooter,
his plan under way.
"I'll discover the truth,
if it takes until May."

The first stop on his journey was the library, of course.
For information and clues this was the source.
"Excuse me, nice lady. I need a few facts."
The startled librarian looked up from the stacks.

"I must know about time and hours and days."
    Oodle stood with his timeometer, his eyes all ablaze.
"Greenwich, England," she said, without batting an eye.
    "That should answer your how, your what and your why."

"In fact, you will find a 'time laboratory,' known through the world as the Royal Observatory."

GREENWICH

HISTORIC SITES
ROYAL OBSERVATORY AND PLANETARIUM

ENGLAND

EUROPE

AFRICA

CANADA

UNITED STATES OF AMERICA

MEXICO

SOUTH AMERICA

The Source of the PRIME MERIDIAN Longitude 0°

"That's your first clue in this mystery time, be on the lookout e special word, '

Off to the airport Oodle shot in a flash,
purchased a ticket and down the aisle dashed.
To reach the small town he must cross the Atlantic.
"The trip will take hours and the jet, it's gigantic!"

TIME FLIES

"It will be a long flight,"
Oodle said with a yawn.
He stared at the night,
but instead he saw dawn.
"It was night when I left.
There must be a mistake. If that is the sun,
well, this takes the cake!"

LONDON SUN TIMES

Prime Minister To Address Parliament

Big Ben

Before he knew it, the plane touched down.
    "I've arrived in Greenwich. It's a seaport town!"
He admired the estate and the air so pure,
    then the Astronomer Royal gave Oodle the tour.

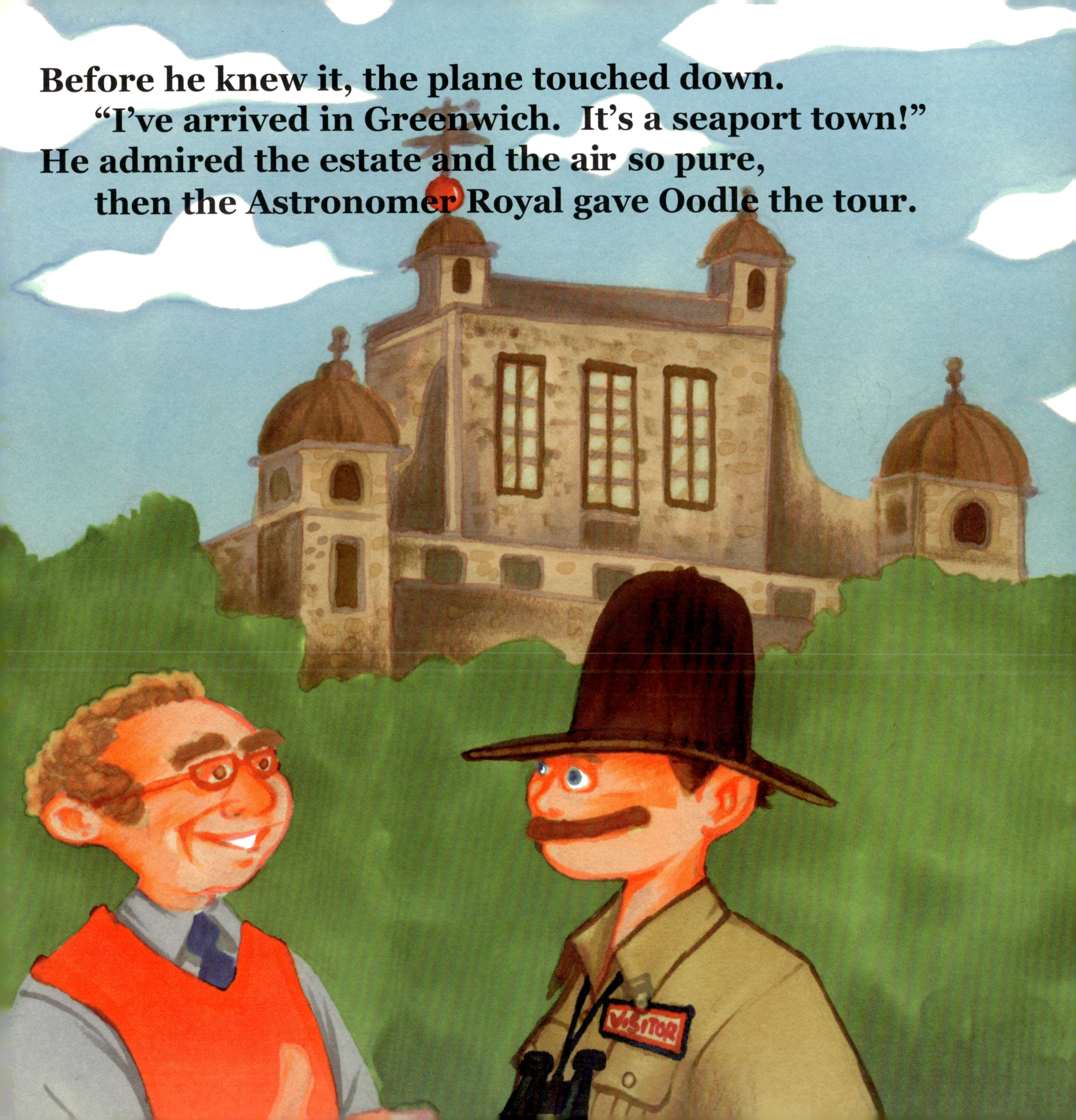

"Time begins here. That is a fact.
     Zero degrees longitude," he stated with tact.
"Longitude lines run north to south on the Earth.
     Latitude lines measure the globe from its girth."

"The prime meridian, that's where we are,
    was calculated and mapped with some distant star."
Oodle straddled the meridian with his time-telling gear.
  "Look at me! I'm in the West and the East Hemisphere!"

"This is fantastic. I must continue my quest,
    and put these longitude lines to the test."
Compass in hand, Oodle travelled 15 degrees east,
    and as he did the hour increased.

15°

He travelled through
Europe,
stopping briefly
in Athens.
"Every 15 degrees,
the same thing
happens.
These longitude lines
keep track
of the time,
just as steady
as my
grandfather chime."

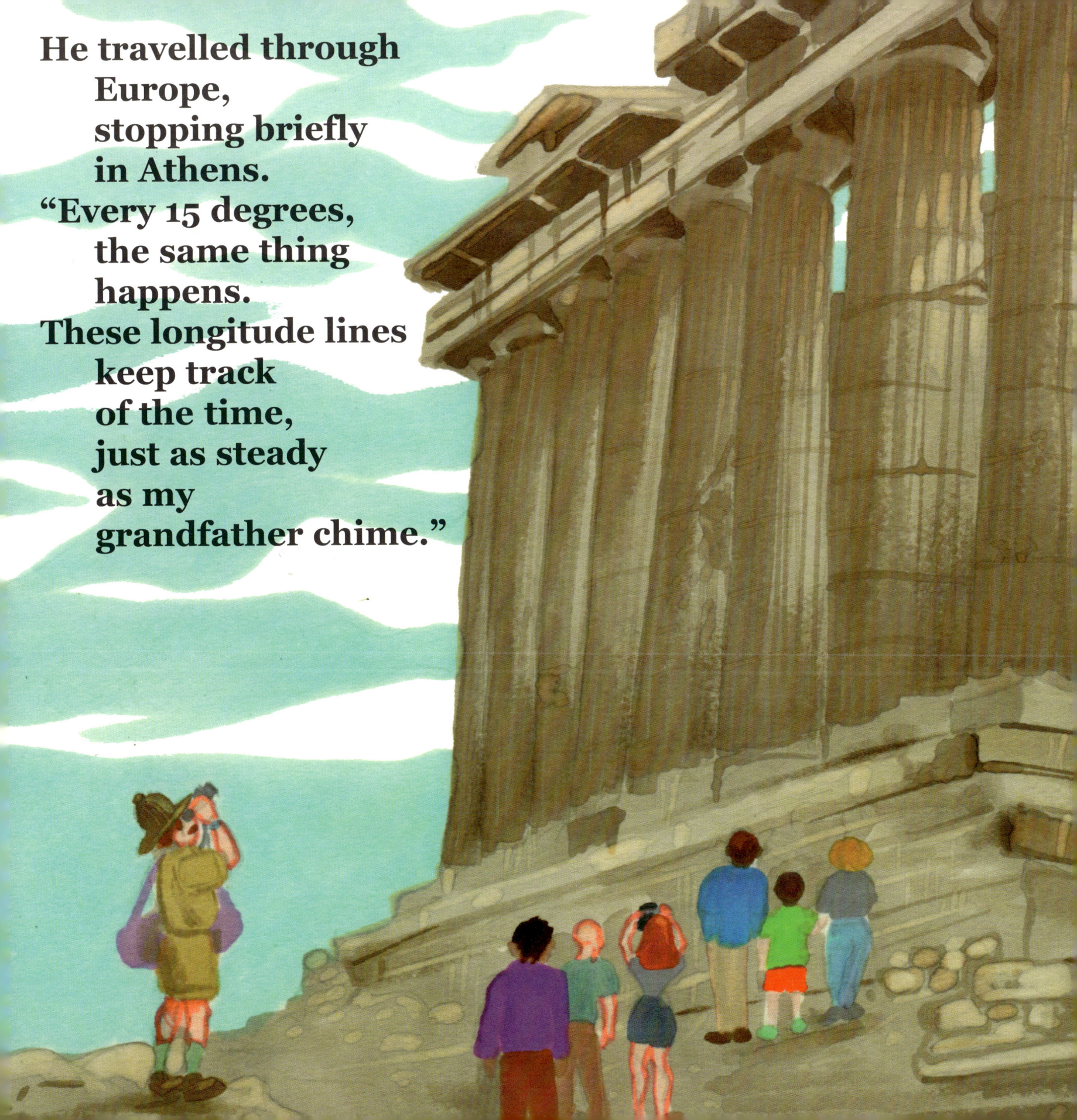

He had travelled quite far in an eastward direction,
when a mystical fellow gave him this suggestion.
"You seem to have time mastered and you understand days,
but I have information that will shock and amaze."

"Travel due north for the riddle's not done.
   You're searching for the Land of the Midnight Sun."
Oodle followed his lead and to the North Pole travelled,
   and that's where his theory came unraveled.

He arrived in the afternoon, but the sun never set.
The later time got the brighter it'd get.
Oodle suspected there was some sort of confusion.
Surely, this had to be an optical illusion.

Igloo
sweet
Igloo

As his new friend talked, the mystery unfurled.
"The reason is simple. We're on top of the world.
It is called the Land of the Midnight Sun,
because from June to July day is not done."

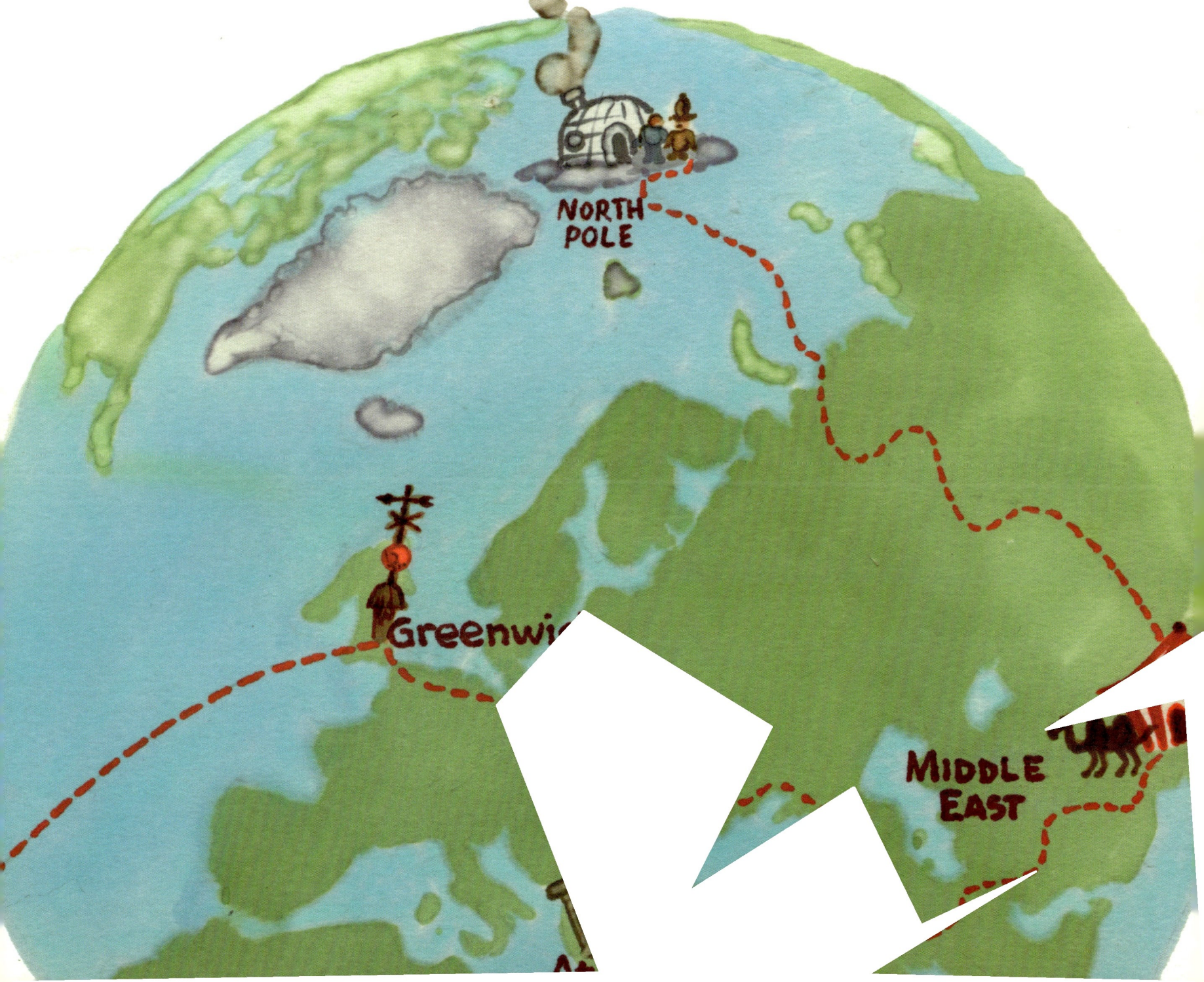

NORTH
POLE

Greenwi

MIDDLE
EAST

"In the middle of winter, we have Arctic nights.
   The only daytime we see is a meager twilight.
And there are some other interesting sights.
   Tonight, we'll experience the Northern Lights."

At midnight Oodle observed the sky all aglow.
How this happened he did not know.
"It's a collision of sorts," the local man grinned.
"The upper atmosphere and the charged solar wind."

Oodle was stunned. It showed on his face.
His thoughts were as tangled as a three-legged race.
"There's something else you must know to get it all straight.
Another place on the globe you must calculate."

Before Oodle knew it he was travelling south,
    and needed something cool for his head and his mouth.
He sipped a tall drink and then, asked a waiter,
    "How much farther to see the equator?"

"Obviously sir, you have not been here before.
  Can't you see you're standing on a tropical shore?"
True, there was a rainforest. And indeed, it was hot.
  Oodle grasped at the concept, but understood it not.

"The equator rounds the center
of this ball called the Earth.
It measures zero degrees latitude,
for what that is worth.
More so than the poles,
the sun strikes right here.
In fact, equatorial regions are hot all year."

An old sea captain rose from his perch.
    "Come with me," said he. "I can help in your search.
There's one big thing to know about the equator.
    It's a North and South Hemisphere separator."

NORTHERN
HEMISPHERE

0°

SOUTHERN
HEMISPHERE

S.S. Dinghy

The captain continued with a tattered old map.
"Forty years on the high seas and not a mishap.
Latitude with longitude helps plot a course.
For sea captains this is an invaluable source."

Oodle zigzagged through Europe.
He touched Pakistan.
He puttered around Russia,
then on to Japan.
After criss-crossing Asia,
he boarded a ship.
Now, for the unusual
part of his trip.

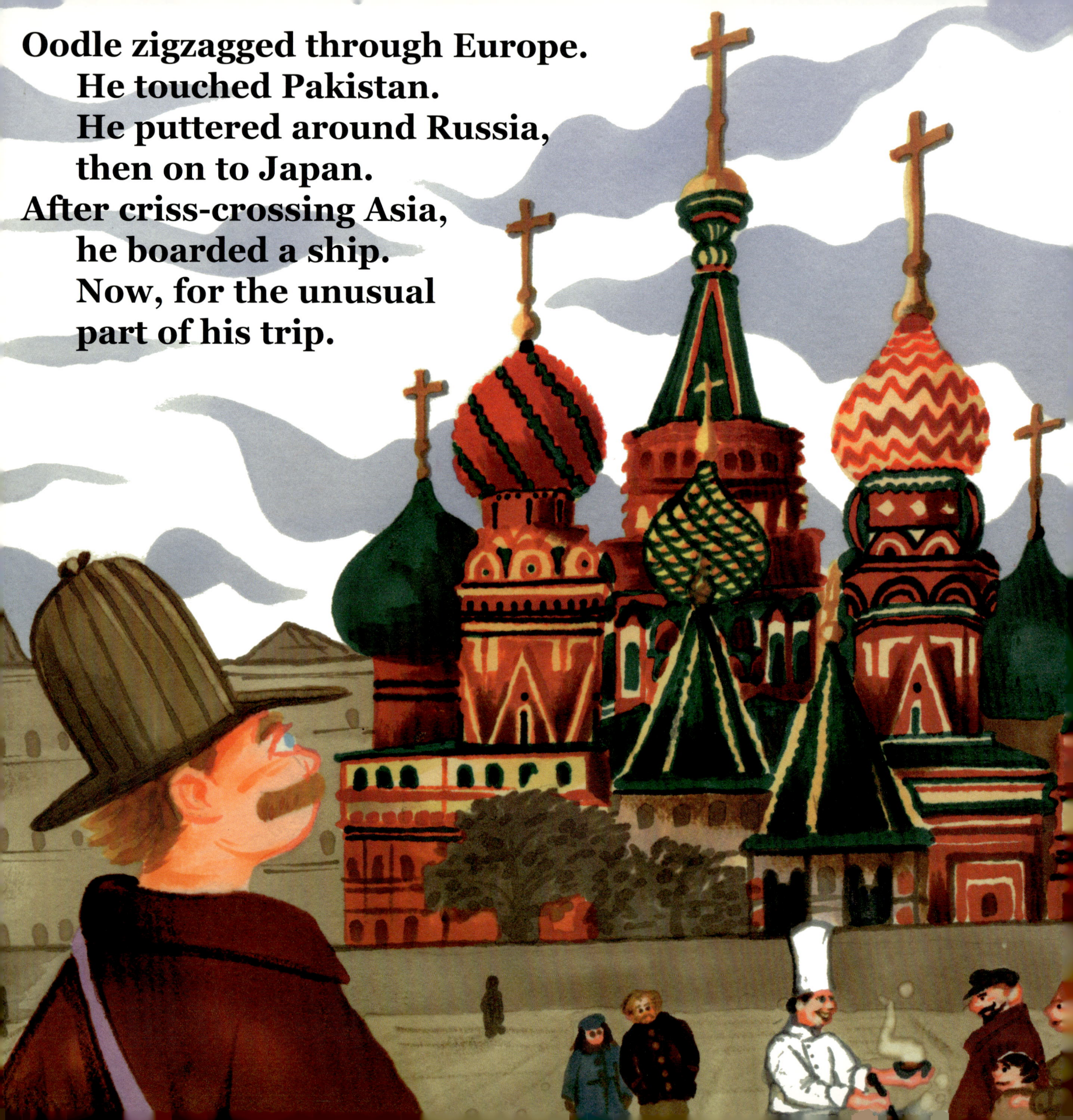

That's where it happened, on the Pacific's high seas,
the mystery at longitude 180 degrees.
He had searched high and low to find the next sign,
then he saw in the water, the international date line.

World Cruise

INTERNATION
DATELINE
LONGITUDE 180°

All over with celebration the ship seemed to burst,
    when the date changed suddenly from the 30th to 1st.
"That's how it happens. Hours increase gradually by one,
    and if you go far enough a new day is begun."

That night as Oodle climbed into his berth,
   he understood the concept of time on this Earth.

But as he covered his head and started to snore,
   a thought crept in of something more.

At times on his journey he needed a sweater,
at other times a swimsuit in the hot, humid weather.
Certainly, he would find explanations and reasons.
"On my next journey I will explore the four seasons."